Quick Bucks: Your Fast-Track Guide to Getting Rich!

Proudly Presented By:

- JWH Jr.

Table of Contents

Quick Bucks:..1
Your Fast-Track Guide to Getting Rich!..........................1
   Introduction:...7
   Chapter 1: The Millionaire Mindset: Think Like a Winner
  12
      Understanding the Millionaire Mindset......................13
      Cultivating a Millionaire Mindset................................16
      Conclusion...19
   Chapter 2: Smart Investments: Putting Your Money to
   Work..20
      Understanding Investments...20
      Building Your Investment Strategy............................22
      Starting Your Investment Journey..............................24
      Conclusion...25
   Chapter 3: Flipping for Profit: Real Estate Strategies that
   Work..25
      What is House Flipping?...26
      Understanding the Market..26
      Finding the Right Property...27
      Renovation Strategies..28
      Selling the Property...29
      Conclusion...30
   Chapter 4: Side Hustles That Pay: Unleashing Your
   Potential...31
      Discovering Your Side Hustle......................................31
      Popular Side Hustle Ideas...32
      Managing Your Side Hustle..34
      Conclusion...35

Chapter 5: Digital Gold: Making Money Online.............36
  Understanding Online Income Streams....................36
  Strategies for Success................................39
  Conclusion..40
Chapter 6: Networking to Wealth: Building Connections that Count...41
  The Importance of Networking..........................41
  Building Your Network.................................42
  Cultivating Relationships.............................44
  Conclusion..44
Chapter 7: Passive Income Streams: Earning While You Sleep...45
  Understanding Passive Income..........................46
  Strategies for Generating Passive Income..............47
  Tips for Success......................................49
  Conclusion..50
Chapter 8: The Art of Negotiation: Getting More for Less 50
  Understanding Negotiation.............................51
  Key Principles of Effective Negotiation...............51
  Negotiation Strategies................................53
  Effective Tactics.....................................54
  Conclusion..55
Chapter 9: Finessing Finances: Budgeting Your Way to Riches..56
  Understanding Budgeting...............................56
  Creating Your Budget..................................57
  Budgeting Strategies..................................58
  Monitoring and Adjusting Your Budget..................59

Conclusion..60
Chapter 10: Tech Trends: Where to Find Your Fortune.61
    Emerging Technology Sectors......................................61
    Navigating the Tech Landscape..................................63
    Conclusion..64
Chapter 11: Mindful Spending: How to Avoid Pitfalls....65
    Understanding Mindful Spending..............................65
    Strategies for Mindful Spending.................................66
    Cultivating a Frugal Mindset.......................................68
    Conclusion..69
Chapter 12: Scaling Up: Turning Small Wins into Big Gains...70
    Understanding the Principle of Scaling Up.................70
    Strategies for Scaling Up..71
    Implementing Effective Scaling Techniques...............73
    Conclusion..74
Chapter 13: The Power of Persistence: Overcoming Challenges..74
    Understanding the Role of Persistence.......................75
    Strategies for Harnessing Persistence........................76
    Building Resilience..77
    Conclusion..78
Chapter 14: Lifestyle Changes for Fast Wealth: What to Do Differently..78
    Understanding the Impact of Lifestyle Choices..........79
    Key Lifestyle Changes for Wealth Building.................80
    Building a Supportive Environment............................81
    Conclusion..82
Chapter 15: Your Financial Future: Setting Goals and Keeping Focused..83

Quick Bucks

The Importance of Setting Financial Goals.................83
Types of Financial Goals..84
Strategies for Effective Goal Setting..........................85
Conclusion..86

Legal Notice:- This Ebook is for informational purposes only. While every attempt has been made to verify the information provided in this Ebook, neither the author nor the distributor assume any responsibility for errors or omissions. Any slights of people or organizations are unintentional and the Development of this Ebook is bona fide. This Ebook has been distributed with the understanding that we are not engaged in rendering technical, legal, accounting or other professional advice. We do not give any kind of guarantee about the accuracy of information provided. In no event will the author and/or marketer be liable for any direct, indirect, incidental, consequential or other loss or damage arising out of the use of this document by any person, regardless of whether or not informed of the possibility of damages in advance.

Introduction:

In a world that seems increasingly dominated by tales of instant wealth and overnight sensations, it's vital to approach the pursuit of riches with a clear strategy and a determined mindset. *Quick Bucks: Your Fast-Track Guide to Getting Rich!* is designed for those who are eager to seize financial independence and prosperity through practical, actionable strategies. Whether you're a student with big dreams, a working professional seeking to boost your income, or someone who's simply tired of living paycheck to paycheck, this book offers the tools and wisdom you need to start building your wealth today.

We live in a time of unprecedented opportunity. The rise of technology and the internet means that more avenues for income exist than ever before. Gone are the days when wealth was confined to a privileged few. With the right mindset, knowledge, and effort, anyone can carve out a fortune. However, it's important to note that this journey won't happen overnight. It requires diligence, patience, and the willingness to learn from failures. The chapters that follow provide step-by-step methodologies, real-world examples, and proven techniques that have helped countless individuals achieve their financial dreams.

The first step to accumulating wealth begins in your mind. The right mindset is crucial; believing that you're able and worthy is the foundation upon which all wealth is built. This book emphasizes the importance of adopting a millionaire mindset—one that embraces positivity, resilience, and an entrepreneurial spirit. When you see challenges as opportunities rather than obstacles, you start to attract the success you desire.

Once your mindset is in place, the practical steps to getting rich become clearer. In *Quick Bucks,* each chapter is meticulously crafted to address various pathways to wealth. You'll learn the power of smart investments, particularly in the ever-evolving world of real estate and stock markets. Each tool and technique is explored with thorough explanations and engaging anecdotes from those who have journeyed down similar paths.

Side hustles are a significant focus in this book. With today's gig economy booming, many opportunities exist to leverage your skills and passions into lucrative side ventures. Whether you're crafting handmade goods to sell online or sharing your expertise through freelance services, the potential to boost your income is limitless.

Moreover, we'll delve into the digital world, where opportunities to make money online can transform your financial status. From e-commerce to blogging, the world is your oyster if you know where to look and how to act.

However, riches aren't solely about making money; they also involve smart money management habits. That's why *Quick Bucks* includes chapters on budgeting and mindful spending, essential strategies for ensuring the money you earn is well-maintained.

Networking can often be overlooked, yet it's critical to wealth-building. You never know which connection may open the door to an incredible opportunity. This book emphasizes the importance of forging valuable relationships in your personal and professional life, showcasing how collaborations can lead to exponential growth in your career trajectory.

As you navigate this journey, there will inevitably be hurdles along the way. But the power of persistence and the right strategies can help you overcome challenges and stay focused on your goals. This book will guide you through mindset shifts and practical steps to adapt, learn from your experiences, and keep moving forward.

Ultimately, *Quick Bucks: Your Fast-Track Guide to Getting Rich!* serves as your roadmap to not just earning more money, but enriching your life with financial knowledge and independence. The pages that follow will empower you to take charge, make informed decisions, and hustle your way to a wealthier future.

Chapter 1: The Millionaire Mindset: Think Like a Winner

Becoming a millionaire begins long before you make your first dollar. It starts with a mindset, a way of thinking that acknowledges the power of wealth and the belief in your potential. The millionaire mindset is characterized by optimism, resilience, and a strong sense of self-worth. It reflects the understanding that financial success isn't just about the numbers—it's about cultivating an internal belief system that empowers you to pursue your dreams relentlessly.

Understanding the Millionaire Mindset

So, what exactly is the millionaire mindset? At its core, it's a collection of beliefs and habits that allow you to see opportunities where others see obstacles. Millionaires think differently; they approach life with curiosity and creativity, leveraging their knowledge and experiences to chart their paths to wealth.

1. **Belief in Abundance:**
   First and foremost, millionaires possess a mindset of abundance. They believe that there are endless opportunities to create wealth and that hard work can lead to reward. This outlook helps them stay motivated and encourages them to take calculated risks. When you believe in abundance, you're less likely to see competition and more likely to see collaboration.

2. **Resilience in the Face of Failure:**
   Every successful entrepreneur has faced setbacks. What differentiates millionaires is their resilience and ability to learn from failures. They understand that failure is a part of the journey to success. Instead of fearing

failure, they embrace it, using each misstep as a lesson to improve and grow.

3. **Growth-Oriented Thinking:**
A millionaire mindset involves continuous learning. Successful individuals are devoted to self-improvement, whether through reading, taking courses, or networking with like-minded people. They understand that knowledge is power and are always looking for ways to expand their skill set. This commitment to personal growth often leads to innovative ideas and opportunities that can be harnessed for financial gain.

4. **Goal Setting and Visualization:**
Millionaires do not wait for success to come to them; they set clear, achievable goals and visualize their paths to success. Writing down specific

objectives—whether they are monthly income goals, savings targets, or milestones in a business venture—creates accountability and a sense of direction. Visualization techniques can also enhance motivation, as picturing yourself reaching those goals makes them feel more attainable.

5. **Disciplined Financial Management:** The way millionaires view money is another key component of their mindset. They prioritize financial literacy and discipline, understanding that every dollar can be an investment in their future. They create budgets, save regularly, and invest wisely, knowing that managing their finances is crucial to long-term wealth accumulation.

Cultivating a Millionaire Mindset

While the millionaire mindset is inherent for some, it can certainly be cultivated through practice and dedication. Here are practical strategies to help you develop this transformational way of thinking:

1. **Daily Affirmations:**
   Start your day with positive affirmations. Statements like "I am capable of achieving financial success" or "Opportunities come my way" can shift your focus toward a success-oriented mindset. Write these affirmations down and repeat them daily until they become ingrained in your subconscious.

2. **Surround Yourself with Like-Minded Individuals:**
   Network with people who share your aspirations and values. Join workshops, seminars, or online groups focused on personal finance and entrepreneurship.

Engaging with motivated individuals will inspire you and provide valuable insights and resources.

3. **Practice Gratitude:**
Cultivating a gratitude practice fosters a positive outlook on life. Start a gratitude journal where you write down things you're thankful for each day. This simple exercise helps shift your focus from scarcity to abundance, enhancing your overall mindset.

4. **Read and Educate Yourself:**
Commit to reading books, articles, and resources on wealth-building, personal finance, and entrepreneurship. Knowledge increases your confidence and equips you with practical tools to navigate your financial journey.

5. **Embrace Challenges:**
Rather than avoiding difficult situations, tackle them head-on. View

challenges as opportunities for growth and learning. Embracing adversity nurtures resilience, making you more adept at handling the inevitable ups and downs that come with building wealth.

6. **Visualize Your Success:**
Spend time visualizing your ideal life and financial situation. Envision achieving your goals and the steps required to get there. This mental exercise enhances motivation and productivity, as it makes your aspirations feel tangible.

Conclusion

Developing a millionaire mindset is not just about accumulating wealth—it's about transforming your overall outlook on life. It begins with believing in yourself, embracing your potential, and equipping yourself with knowledge and resilience to navigate the world of wealth creation.

In the following chapters, we will explore the practical steps that align with this mindset, empowering you to take action and work towards your financial dreams. The journey begins now; let's dive into the world of smart investments and wealth creation strategies that will set you on the path to financial freedom.

Chapter 2: Smart Investments: Putting Your Money to Work

In today's fast-paced world, simply saving money isn't sufficient to build wealth. The key to financial growth lies in investing. This chapter will explore the various investment strategies that can accelerate your wealth-building efforts. More than just a good habit, investing is the cornerstone of financial independence.

Understanding Investments

1. What is Investing?
Investing entails putting your money into assets with the expectation of generating a return. Unlike saving, which typically only provides modest interest, investing allows your money to grow in value over time, leveraging the power of compounding interest.

2. Types of Investments:
Investments come in various forms, each with its own risk and return profiles. The primary categories include:

- **Stocks:** When you buy stock, you purchase a share (a small part) of a company. Stocks can provide high returns, but they also carry greater risk. You can earn money through price appreciation and dividends.

- **Bonds:** Bonds are essentially loans you give to companies or governments in exchange for periodic interest payments and the return of the bond's face value when it matures. They are generally considered safer than stocks.

- **Mutual Funds and ETFs:** These investment vehicles pool money from many investors to purchase a diversified portfolio of stocks and/or bonds, allowing for diversification and professional management.

- **Real Estate:** Investing in property can produce rental income and appreciable value over time. Real estate is often seen as a stable investment and a good hedge against inflation.

- **Commodities:** Investments in physical goods like gold, oil, or agricultural products can serve as a hedge against market fluctuations. Commodities can be volatile but offer diversification.

Building Your Investment Strategy

1. Determine Your Investment Goals:
Before investing, assess what you aim to achieve—be it saving for retirement, purchasing a home, or funding a child's education. Your goals will influence your investment strategy.

2. Assess Your Risk Tolerance:
Understanding your risk tolerance is crucial. Are you comfortable with fluctuations in your investment value? Generally, younger investors can take on more risk since they have time to recover from market downturns. Older investors may prefer safer, more stable investments.

3. Diversify Your Portfolio:
Don't put all your eggs in one basket.

Diversification minimizes risk by spreading investments across various asset classes to reduce the impact of poor performance in any one area.

4. Invest for the Long-Term:
Successful investors often take a long-term perspective. While short-term trading can yield quick profits, it can also result in significant losses. A long-term strategy allows you to ride out market volatility and benefit from compounding returns.

Starting Your Investment Journey

1. Open an Investment Account:
To begin investing, you'll need to set up an investment account. Brokerage firms offer platforms for buying and selling investments, often with user-friendly online tools.

2. Start Small:
You don't need a large sum of money to

start investing. Consider starting with a modest amount and gradually increasing your investment as you become more comfortable.

3. Utilize Dollar-Cost Averaging:
This strategy involves regularly investing a fixed amount of money, regardless of market conditions. Over time, this can help mitigate volatility and reduce the impact of market fluctuations.

4. Keep Learning:
Investing requires knowledge and staying informed about market trends, economic indicators, and investment strategies. Continuously educate yourself through books, podcasts, and financial news.

Conclusion

Investing is a powerful tool for building wealth and should be a key component of your financial strategy. By understanding different types of investments and finding a strategy that aligns with your goals and risk tolerance, you can put your money to work and pave the way for a financially secure future. In the next chapter, we will dive into real estate investing and explore strategies that work in today's market.

Chapter 3: Flipping for Profit: Real Estate Strategies that Work

Real estate investing is one of the most powerful ways to build wealth, and flipping properties offers an exciting path with the potential for significant profits. This chapter delves into the intricacies of flipping houses, outlining practical steps and strategies to maximize your success in the real estate market.

What is House Flipping?

House flipping involves buying a property (often below market value), renovating it, and selling it for a profit. While it may seem simple, successful flipping requires careful planning, thorough research, and market knowledge.

Understanding the Market

1. Research Local Markets:
Before diving into flipping, study local property markets to identify desirable neighborhoods and price trends. Markets may fluctuate based on economic conditions, demographics, and community development.

2. Identify Market Trends:
Analyze real estate trends to determine what buyers want. Features like modern kitchens, open floor plans, and energy-efficient appliances may attract buyers, positively influencing resale value.

Finding the Right Property

1. Set a Budget:
Determine your budget, including purchase price, renovation costs, and selling costs. Stick to your budget to avoid potential pitfalls that can erode profits.

2. Look for Undervalued Properties:
Find properties below market value—foreclosures, distressed homes, or properties needing minor repairs can be excellent opportunities. Use online real estate listings, auctions, and networking to locate promising deals.

3. Conduct Due Diligence:
Once a property catches your eye, conduct thorough inspections to identify any potential issues. Engaging a professional inspector can help uncover hidden problems, ensuring you're not blindsided by costly repairs later.

Renovation Strategies

1. Prioritize Renovations:
Focus on renovations that offer the most return for your investment. Regular updates to kitchens, bathrooms, and curb appeal often yield significant returns. Open floor plans and energy-efficient installations are hot commodities.

2. Manage Your Time and Costs:
Prepare a realistic timeline and stick to it. Delays can incur higher costs for holding the property longer. Hire trusted contractors or consider taking on minor renovations yourself to save money.

3. Keep a Budget Tracker:
Keep meticulous records of all expenses related to renovations. This track of costs can help you evaluate profitability once the property is sold.

Selling the Property

1. Staging the Home:
Once renovations are complete, consider staging the home to highlight its best features. A well-staged home can evoke emotional responses from buyers and lead to quicker, higher offers.

2. Set a Competitive Price:
Analyze comparable properties in the market to set a competitive selling price. Pricing too high may drive potential buyers away, while pricing too low can undermine your profits.

3. Market Effectively:
Utilize multiple platforms to market your property. Social media, real estate websites, and local listings can help maximize exposure. Don't underestimate the value of open houses!

4. Negotiate Smartly:
Be prepared to negotiate offers. Understand the market, your property's value, and

remain firm yet flexible in discussions to achieve a fair deal.

Conclusion

House flipping can be a lucrative venture when approached with knowledge, strategy, and persistence. Thorough research and effective project management are crucial to your success. In the following chapter, we will explore various side hustles that can supplement your income as you work towards your financial goals.

Chapter 4: Side Hustles That Pay: Unleashing Your Potential

In today's gig economy, side hustles have become a popular way to boost income and enhance financial security. Whether you're looking to pay off debt, save for a major purchase, or simply increase your earnings, a side hustle can provide additional cash flow and opportunities for new skills and experiences. This chapter will explore various side hustles, highlighting strategies to leverage your skills and interests for financial gain.

Discovering Your Side Hustle

1. Identify Your Skills and Interests: Reflect on your hobbies, talents, and expertise. What are you passionate about? What skills can you offer to others? Identifying areas of interest ensures that your side hustle remains enjoyable and sustainable.

2. Analyze Market Demand: Research what services or products people are willing to pay for. Marketplace trends can provide insight into lucrative opportunities. Websites like Upwork and

Fiverr can help gauge demand for skills relevant to your expertise.

Popular Side Hustle Ideas

1. Freelancing:
If you have skills in writing, graphic design, marketing, or programming, consider freelancing. Platforms like Upwork, Fiverr, and Freelancer allow you to connect with clients looking for your skill set.

2. Online Tutoring:
If you have knowledge in a particular subject, tutoring can be a fulfilling side hustle. Websites like Chegg and Tutor.com connect tutors with students needing assistance.

3. E-commerce:
Leverage platforms like Etsy, eBay, and Amazon to sell handmade items, vintage goods, or dropship products. E-commerce

allows you to reach a broad audience and generate income from your creativity.

4. Blogging or Vlogging:
If you're passionate about a topic, consider starting a blog or YouTube channel. While it may take time to build an audience, monetization options such as affiliate marketing, sponsorships, and ads can yield profitable returns.

5. Ride-sharing or Delivery Services:
Utilize your vehicle to earn extra money by driving for services like Uber, Lyft, DoorDash, or Postmates. These platforms offer flexible schedules, allowing you to work when it suits you.

6. Pet Sitting or Dog Walking:
If you love animals, consider pet sitting or dog walking. Websites like Rover and Wag allow you to connect with pet owners in your area seeking pet care.

7. Rent Out a Room or Property:
If you have extra space, consider renting it out on platforms like Airbnb. Short-term rentals can provide significant income, especially in high-demand areas.

Managing Your Side Hustle

1. Set a Schedule:
Establish a clear schedule that balances your side hustle with your main job and personal life. Effective time management ensures consistency and prevents burnout.

2. Stay Organized:
Use tools like spreadsheets or apps to track income and expenses related to your side hustle. Monitoring your progress can help motivate you and set achievable goals.

3. Market Your Services:
Promote your side hustle through social media, networking, and word of mouth.

Building a strong online presence can help attract clients.

4. Continuously Improve Skills:
Invest in personal development through online courses or workshops relevant to your side hustle. Enhancing your skills can lead to higher-paying opportunities and better results.

Conclusion

Side hustles offer a valuable path to financial growth and independence. By leveraging your skills and passions, you can create additional income streams that enhance your overall financial picture. In the next chapter, we will explore the digital realm and discuss how to make money online through various ventures.

Chapter 5: Digital Gold: Making Money Online

The digital age has transformed how we earn money, creating a myriad of opportunities to generate income online. From e-commerce to passive income streams, the internet provides endless possibilities to build wealth. This chapter will explore various avenues to make money online, emphasizing strategies that can maximize your earning potential.

Understanding Online Income Streams

1. E-commerce:
Running an online store has never been easier. Platforms like Shopify, WooCommerce, and Etsy allow you to create a storefront with minimal upfront investment. You can sell physical products, digital downloads, or even dropship items. The key is understanding your target

market and leveraging effective marketing strategies.

2. Affiliate Marketing:

Affiliate marketing allows you to earn commissions by promoting products or services through your unique referral links. You can promote these links via a blog, social media, or email newsletters. Successful affiliate marketers typically cultivate a niche audience that trusts their recommendations.

3. Blogging or Vlogging:

Creating engaging content can attract a wide audience and monetize your platform through ads, sponsorships, and merchandise sales. Focus on topics you're passionate about and provide value to your audience to grow your following. Consistency, quality, and search engine optimization (SEO) are vital to success in this realm.

4. Online Courses or E-books:

If you possess expertise in a particular field, consider creating online courses or e-books. Platforms like Teachable and Udemy make it easy to share your knowledge and generate passive income. Focus on delivering value and actionable insights to your audience.

5. Remote Work:

Many companies now offer remote work opportunities, allowing you to earn a salary while working from home or anywhere with internet access. Websites like Remote.co and We Work Remotely list various remote job listings across industries.

Strategies for Success

1. Build an Online Presence:

Develop a professional website and establish a strong social media presence to enhance credibility and attract potential clients or customers. Regularly publish quality content and engage with your audience to build a loyal following.

2. Leverage SEO and Marketing:
Implementing effective digital marketing strategies, including search engine optimization (SEO), can enhance your online visibility. Understand how to attract organic traffic to your website or content, boosting your chances of making sales or generating leads.

3. Stay Informed and Adapt:
The online landscape is constantly evolving. Stay updated about trends, tools, and technologies relevant to your field. Adapt your strategies accordingly to remain competitive and maximize your potential.

4. Focus on Building Relationships:
Whether you're working with affiliates, clients, or customers, cultivating strong relationships can lead to repeat business

and collaborative opportunities. Offer exceptional service and value to build trust.

Conclusion

The digital world is a land of opportunity for those willing to invest time and effort. By leveraging your skills and interests, you can establish a successful online income stream that empowers your financial goals. In the next chapter, we will explore the importance of networking and building valuable connections that can lead to wealth.

Chapter 6: Networking to Wealth: Building Connections that Count

Networking is one of the most effective tools for building wealth. The relationships you cultivate can open doors to new opportunities, collaborations, and invaluable resources. This chapter will explore the power of networking and provide strategies to build your network effectively, positioning you to achieve your financial goals.

The Importance of Networking

1. Opportunities and Referrals:
Networking can lead to job offers, business partnerships, and investment opportunities. Building a strong network often generates referrals, helping you tap into potential clients.

2. Knowledge and Support:
Connecting with others fosters knowledge sharing and collaboration. Your network can provide insights, advice, and a different perspective when facing challenges.

3. Credibility and Reputation:
A solid network can enhance your professional reputation. Being connected to

respected individuals or organizations can increase your credibility and trust within your industry.

Building Your Network

1. Attend Networking Events:
Participate in industry conferences, seminars, and workshops. These gatherings provide opportunities to meet like-minded individuals, learn from experts, and broaden your network.

2. Join Professional Organizations:
Become a member of professional organizations related to your field. These groups often host events, webinars, and online forums, creating spaces for networking and collaboration.

3. Leverage Social Media:
Platforms like LinkedIn, Twitter, and Facebook can connect you with professionals in your industry. Regularly

engage in discussions, share valuable content, and connect with individuals who align with your goals.

4. Offer Value:
When networking, focus on how you can provide value to others. Whether through sharing insights, resources, or connections, reciprocity is essential in building meaningful relationships.

5. Follow Up:
After meeting someone, send a follow-up message expressing gratitude and interest in staying connected. Personalizing your outreach can strengthen your relationship and keep you top-of-mind.

Cultivating Relationships

1. Be Genuine:
Authenticity is key to meaningful connections. Show real interest in others

and seek to understand their goals, challenges, and experiences.

2. Stay in Touch:
Building a network is about maintaining relationships. Make an effort to check in periodically, share relevant information, and celebrate others' successes.

3. Collaborate:
Look for opportunities to collaborate with individuals in your network. Joint ventures, projects, or partnerships can lead to mutually beneficial outcomes.

Conclusion

Networking is a powerful wealth-building tool that can significantly impact your financial trajectory. By cultivating valuable connections and fostering authentic relationships, you position yourself for opportunities that may otherwise remain undiscovered. In the next chapter, we will discuss passive income strategies to create additional streams of revenue while you sleep.

Chapter 7: Passive Income Streams: Earning While You Sleep

As you build your wealth, creating streams of passive income can be a game-changer. Passive income allows you to earn money without continuous active involvement, freeing up your time for other pursuits. This chapter will explore various strategies for developing passive income streams that can enhance your financial security.

Understanding Passive Income

1. What is Passive Income?
Passive income is earned with minimal effort after the initial work is completed. Unlike active income, which requires

ongoing work (like a traditional job), passive income can flow in regularly once established.

2. Benefits of Passive Income:

- **Financial Security:** Multiple income streams provide financial stability, reducing reliance on a single source.
- **Time Freedom:** Passive income allows you to redirect time toward other interests, investments, or personal projects.
- **Potential for Scalability:** Many passive income opportunities can be scaled, allowing you to increase your earnings over time.

Strategies for Generating Passive Income

1. Real Estate Investments:
Investing in rental properties can provide a consistent passive income stream. By

leasing out properties, you can earn monthly rent without the need to actively manage the property.

2. Dividend Stocks:
Investing in dividend-paying stocks allows you to earn income through regular dividend payments. Focus on companies with a history of stable or increasing dividends for reliable returns.

3. Peer-to-Peer Lending:
Platforms like LendingClub allow you to lend money to individuals or small businesses in exchange for interest payments. This strategy requires careful assessment of risk but can yield attractive returns.

4. Create an Online Course:
Developing online courses based on your expertise can generate passive income. Once created, you can sell your course on

platforms like Udemy or Teachable, earning money while you sleep.

5. Write a Book or E-book:
If you have knowledge to share, consider writing a book or e-book. Once published, you can earn royalties from sales without ongoing effort.

6. Build an Online Business:
Creating a dropshipping business or affiliate marketing site allows you to earn money passively. Although initial setup requires effort, it can lead to ongoing income with minimal maintenance.

7. Create a YouTube Channel:
Once established, a YouTube channel can generate income through ads, sponsorships, and merchandise sales. Providing valuable content can attract a loyal audience.

Tips for Success

1. Do Your Research:
Before venturing into any passive income stream, conduct thorough research to understand the risks, potential returns, and market dynamics.

2. Be Patient:
Building passive income takes time and effort upfront. Stay committed, and be prepared for the long haul to reap the rewards.

3. Diversify Your Income Sources:
Don't rely on a single passive income stream. Diversifying your investments and income sources can mitigate risk and increase your overall financial security.

4. Monitor and Optimize:
Even passive income requires occasional attention. Review your investments, assess performance, and make adjustments as needed to maximize returns.

Conclusion

Establishing passive income streams can significantly enhance your financial situation and provide more freedom in your life. By focusing on a diversified portfolio of passive income-generating activities, you can build sustainable wealth. In the next chapter, we will explore the art of negotiation and how effective negotiation skills can help you get more for less in both personal and professional contexts.

Chapter 8: The Art of Negotiation: Getting More for Less

Negotiation is a fundamental skill that can dramatically impact your financial success. Whether negotiating a salary, closing a business deal, or securing discounts, mastering negotiation techniques can help you achieve better outcomes. This chapter will explore the essential principles of negotiation and practical strategies to enhance your skills.

Understanding Negotiation

1. What is Negotiation?
Negotiation is the process of discussing an agreement between two or more parties. It involves communication, persuasion, and compromise to reach a mutually beneficial outcome.

2. Importance of Negotiation:
Negotiation skills are vital in business and personal finance. Effective negotiators can secure better deals, increase salaries, lower costs, and build valuable relationships.

Key Principles of Effective Negotiation

1. Know Your Goals:
Before entering any negotiation, clarify what you want to achieve. Define your

objectives, ideal outcomes, and acceptable compromises.

2. Do Your Research:
Gather information about the other party, their needs, and market standards. Understanding the context and background can give you leverage during negotiations.

3. Build Rapport:
Establishing a positive relationship can enhance negotiation outcomes. Start discussions on friendly terms, listen actively, and strive to understand the other party's perspective.

4. Be Clear and Assertive:
Communicate your needs and expectations clearly and confidently. Avoid being aggressive but assert your position respectfully, showing that you know your worth.

Negotiation Strategies

1. Prepare and Practice:
Preparation is key to successful negotiations. Role-play scenarios, rehearse your points, and anticipate objections. The more prepared you are, the more confidently you can engage in discussions.

2. Use the "BATNA" Approach:
BATNA stands for "Best Alternative to a Negotiated Agreement." Knowing your alternatives gives you leverage and confidence in discussions. If the negotiation doesn't go as planned, having a backup option can help you avoid settling for less.

3. Listen Actively:
Listening is a critical aspect of negotiation. Pay attention to the other party's words, tone, and body language. By understanding their concerns, you can address them effectively and find common ground.

4. Focus on Win-Win Solutions:
Aim for outcomes that benefit both parties.

Negotiations that consider the interests of all involved create stronger relationships and increase the likelihood of future collaborations.

Effective Tactics

1. Start High:
When negotiating, start with a higher offer or request. This establishes your expectations and provides room for negotiation, allowing you to work towards a more favorable outcome.

2. Use Silence:
Silence can be a powerful negotiation tactic. After making a request or offer, pause and let the other party consider. This tactic can lead to pressure on them to respond positively.

3. Be Willing to Walk Away:
Sometimes, the best negotiation strategy is to be prepared to walk away if your needs

aren't met. This demonstrates confidence in your worth and can prompt the other party to reconsider their position.

Conclusion

Mastering the art of negotiation can lead to better deals, increased earning potential, and improved relationships in personal and professional endeavors. By honing your negotiation skills, you position yourself to achieve more for less. In the next chapter, we will explore budgeting strategies that help you effectively manage your finances as you work towards your wealth-building goals.

Chapter 9: Finessing Finances: Budgeting Your Way to Riches

Budgeting is a crucial aspect of financial success, enabling you to effectively track and manage your income. A well-structured budget provides a roadmap for achieving your financial goals and serves as the foundation for wealth-building. This chapter will explore effective budgeting strategies and tips to help you take control of your finances.

Understanding Budgeting

1. What is Budgeting?

Budgeting is the process of creating a plan for how to spend your money. It involves monitoring income and expenses, allocating funds to various categories, and ensuring you live within your means.

2. Importance of Budgeting:

- **Financial Awareness:** Budgeting helps you understand your spending habits, identifying areas for improvement or savings.

- **Control Over Finances:** By establishing a budget, you take control of your money rather than letting it control you.
- **Goal Achievement:** A budget allows you to allocate resources towards specific financial goals, such as saving for a home, paying off debt, or investing.

Creating Your Budget

1. Track Your Income and Expenses: Begin by assessing your income sources, including salary, side hustles, or passive income. Next, document all monthly expenses, including rent, utilities, groceries, and discretionary spending.

2. Categorize Your Expenses: Divide your expenses into fixed (unchanging costs, like rent) and variable (fluctuating costs, like dining out). This helps identify where you can adjust spending.

3. Set Financial Goals:
Establish short-term and long-term financial goals. Whether it's saving a specific amount for a vacation or retirement, clearly defined goals dictate how to allocate resources.

4. Allocate Funds:
Based on your income and goals, designate funds for each category. Allocate essentials first, then allocate funds to your savings and discretionary spending.

Budgeting Strategies

1. The 50/30/20 Rule:
This popular budgeting method recommends allocating 50% of your income to needs (essentials), 30% to wants (discretionary spending), and 20% to savings and debt repayment. This simple

structure can help many achieve a balanced financial approach.

2. Zero-Based Budgeting:
In a zero-based budget, every dollar of income is assigned a specific purpose, resulting in a net income of zero at the end of the month. This method emphasizes intentional spending and can curb waste.

3. Envelope System:
This cash-based budgeting method involves dividing cash into envelopes for each expense category. When the envelope is empty, you cannot spend in that category until the next budget period, encouraging mindful spending.

Monitoring and Adjusting Your Budget

1. Regular Review:
Schedule monthly or quarterly budget reviews. Assess your spending patterns and

evaluate whether you stay on track with your financial goals.

2. Adjust as Needed:
Life circumstances change, and so may your financial situation. Adjust your budget to reflect changes in income, expenses, or goals. Adapting ensures you remain aligned with your financial objectives.

Conclusion

Budgeting is the cornerstone of financial literacy and stability. By creating a detailed budget that reflects your goals and lifestyle, you can take control of your finances and pave the way for wealth accumulation. In the next chapter, we will explore emerging tech trends and innovative industries where you can find your fortune.

Chapter 10: Tech Trends: Where to Find Your Fortune

As technology continues to revolutionize our world, numerous opportunities emerge for savvy investors and entrepreneurs. Understanding current tech trends can position you to capitalize on innovative industries, creating wealth and success. This chapter will examine emerging technologies and industries and how to navigate the thrilling future landscape.

Emerging Technology Sectors

1. Artificial Intelligence (AI):
AI is transforming industries from healthcare to finance, creating opportunities for investment and innovation. Understanding AI applications can lead to investments in companies developing cutting-edge technologies or starting businesses that utilize AI for efficiency.

2. Blockchain and Cryptocurrencies:
Blockchain technology is reshaping finance, supply chains, and security.
Cryptocurrencies like Bitcoin and Ethereum present investment opportunities, though accompanied by volatility and regulation risks. Researching the fundamentals of blockchain technology can position you to capitalize on this disruptive innovation.

3. E-commerce Growth:
The e-commerce sector continues to grow as consumers shift towards online shopping. Investing in e-commerce startups or building an online store can yield profitable returns in this rapidly expanding market.

4. Renewable Energy:
As the world transitions to sustainable energy sources, industries like solar and wind power present opportunities for investment and entrepreneurial ventures. Understanding the renewable energy

landscape can lead to lucrative projects that align with global sustainability goals.

5. Remote Work Solutions:
With more companies adopting remote work policies, there is a rising demand for tools that facilitate collaboration and productivity. Investing in platforms or creating services that cater to remote work can meet a growing market need.

Navigating the Tech Landscape

1. Research and Educate Yourself:
Stay informed about technological advancements and trends in your areas of interest. Regular reading, attending workshops, and engaging with online communities can enhance your understanding of emerging technologies.

2. Networking Opportunities:
Connect with professionals and entrepreneurs within the tech space.

Networking events, online forums, and industry conferences provide valuable insights and potential collaboration opportunities.

3. Identify Gaps in the Market:
Analyze current tech solutions and identify pain points or inefficiencies. Innovations that address existing market gaps have the potential for significant success.

4. Develop a Business Plan:
If considering entrepreneurship, develop a solid business plan outlining your concept, target market, financial projections, and growth strategies. A well-thought-out plan can attract investors and provide clear direction.

Conclusion

The technology landscape offers a wealth of opportunities for investors and entrepreneurs alike. By staying informed, leveraging tech trends, and pursuing innovative ideas, you can navigate this exciting landscape and potentially build wealth while contributing to the future of industries poised for success. In the next chapter, we will explore mindful spending and how to cultivate a frugal mindset to avoid common financial pitfalls.

Chapter 11: Mindful Spending: How to Avoid Pitfalls

In the quest for financial independence, mindful spending is essential. Being conscious of your purchasing decisions allows you to align your spending with your values and financial goals. This chapter will explore strategies for avoiding common financial pitfalls and cultivating a frugal yet fulfilling lifestyle.

Understanding Mindful Spending

1. What is Mindful Spending?

Mindful spending involves being intentional and conscious of your financial decisions. Instead of mindlessly purchasing items, you evaluate each decision based on your values and financial goals.

2. Importance of Mindful Spending:

- **Financial Control:** Mindful spending empowers you to take charge of your financial situation, ensuring spending aligns with your priorities.
- **Reduced Debt:** By avoiding impulse purchases, you minimize unnecessary debt and expenses that can hinder your wealth-building efforts.
- **Increased Savings:** Mindful spending encourages savings and investment over extravagance, promoting financial growth.

Strategies for Mindful Spending

1. Create a Spending Plan:
Develop a clear spending plan that outlines essential categories and budget allocations. Stick to this plan when making purchases to avoid overspending.

2. Practice the 24-Hour Rule:
Before making a non-essential purchase, wait 24 hours. This cooling-off period allows you to evaluate whether the purchase aligns with your values and goals.

3. Distinguish Between Needs and Wants:
Evaluate the necessity of each purchase. Needs are essential for daily living, while wants are discretionary. Prioritize spending on essential items and evaluate the necessity of wants.

4. Use Cash or Debit:
Using cash or a debit card can help limit spending compared to credit cards. When you physically see the money leaving your

hands, you're more likely to be mindful of your purchases.

5. Track Your Spending:
Maintain a journal or use apps to log your expenses. Regularly reviewing your spending habits can highlight areas of overspending and guide adjustments.

Cultivating a Frugal Mindset

1. Embrace Minimalism:
Consider adopting a minimalist mindset by decluttering your life. Focus on quality over quantity, investing in fewer, higher-quality items that truly add value to your life.

2. Seek Alternatives:
Explore free or low-cost alternatives for entertainment, dining, or leisure activities. Engaging in community events, outdoor activities, or home-cooked meals can promote enjoyment without straining your budget.

3. Set Savings Goals:

Establish specific savings goals, whether for emergency funds, travel, or investments. Having tangible objectives can motivate you to spend mindfully and prioritize saving.

4. Celebrate Achievements:

Recognize and celebrate your achievements, whether it's saving a certain amount or sticking to your budget. Acknowledging your progress reinforces positive financial habits.

Conclusion

Mindful spending is a powerful practice that can significantly impact your financial well-being. By aligning your spending habits with your values and financial objectives, you can avoid pitfalls and foster a lifestyle that supports wealth-building and financial success. In the next chapter, we will discuss scaling up your efforts, transforming small wins into significant gains on your path to financial success.

Chapter 12: Scaling Up: Turning Small Wins into Big Gains

In the journey to wealth, scaling up your efforts is vital. Small wins can accumulate over time, leading to substantial financial growth when executed strategically. This chapter will explore how to leverage small victories to scale up your financial endeavors and achieve significant gains.

Understanding the Principle of Scaling Up

1. What Does Scaling Up Mean?
Scaling up means increasing your efforts, resources, or investments to amplify your results. In finance, it involves taking small

wins and leveraging them to create greater returns.

2. Importance of Scaling Up:

- **Exponential Growth:** Scaling up allows for compound growth. Small victories can snowball into larger successes when consistently applied.
- **Increased Opportunities:** Expanding your efforts opens doors to new opportunities, partnerships, and revenue streams.
- **Building Momentum:** Achieving small wins builds confidence and momentum, further fueling your pursuit of larger financial goals.

Strategies for Scaling Up

1. Reinvest Profits:
If you earn income from investments, consider reinvesting those profits. This

strategy accelerates growth over time, compounding your wealth.

2. Diversify Your Income Sources:
Don't rely solely on one income stream. Explore side hustles, investments, or passive income opportunities to create a diversified portfolio that enhances financial stability.

3. Enhance Your Skills:
Invest in personal development and skill enhancement to increase your earning potential. Acquiring new skills can lead to promotions, higher-paying job opportunities, or more lucrative side hustle options.

4. Set Bigger Goals:
Once you achieve small wins, aim higher. Establish progressively challenging financial goals that stretch your capabilities, pushing you to scale up your efforts.

Implementing Effective Scaling Techniques

1. Automate Savings and Investments:
Set up automatic transfers to savings and investment accounts. Automating your finances minimizes the temptation to spend and facilitates consistent growth.

2. Utilize Technology:
Leverage technology and tools to streamline your financial processes. Investing in apps or platforms that help you manage investments, budgeting, or savings can enhance efficiency and results.

3. Collaborate with Others:
Seek partnerships or collaborations that can amplify your efforts. Collaborating with others can lead to new ideas, expanded resources, and accelerated growth.

4. Monitor and Evaluate Progress:
Regularly assess your progress towards scaling up. Evaluate what strategies are

working and make necessary adjustments to ensure you're aligned with your goals.

Conclusion

Scaling up your financial efforts is essential for transforming small wins into substantial gains. By leveraging resources, investing profits, and continuously evolving your strategies, you can enhance your wealth-building journey. In the next chapter, we will delve into the power of persistence and how to overcome challenges as you work towards your financial ambitions.

Chapter 13: The Power of Persistence: Overcoming Challenges

Building wealth is not a linear process; it's filled with ups and downs, risks, and triumphs. The key to navigating this journey is persistence. This chapter will explore the power of persistence and how to overcome challenges as you work towards achieving your financial ambitions.

Understanding the Role of Persistence

1. What is Persistence?
Persistence is the quality of continuing steadfastly despite difficulties or opposition. It's the refusal to give up when faced with obstacles or setbacks.

2. Importance of Persistence in Wealth Building:

- **Overcoming Obstacles:** Persistence equips you with the resilience to face challenges and navigate the inevitable ups and downs of wealth building.
- **Achieving Long-Term Goals:** Financial success often requires sustained effort over time. Persistence is crucial for achieving long-term financial goals.

Strategies for Harnessing Persistence

1. Set Realistic Goals:
Establish clear, achievable financial goals. Break down larger objectives into manageable steps to create a sense of accomplishment as you progress.

2. Stay Focused on Your Why:
Understanding the reasons behind your financial goals can fuel your motivation. Reflect on what drives your desire for wealth—whether it's financial freedom, security for your family, or pursuing a passion—and use it as a guiding force.

3. Learn from Setbacks:
Rather than viewing setbacks as failures, embrace them as opportunities for lessons. Analyzing what went wrong can provide insights that help you navigate future challenges more effectively.

4. Surround Yourself with Support:
Connect with like-minded individuals who inspire and support your journey. Whether through networking or mentorship, surrounding yourself with positive influences can bolster your persistence.

Building Resilience

1. Develop a Positive Mindset:
Cultivating a positive mindset can help you maintain persistence in the face of difficulties. Focus on solutions rather than problems, and practice gratitude to shift your perspective.

2. Embrace Continuous Learning:
Financial landscapes change, and continuous learning equips you to adapt. Invest time in reading, taking courses, or seeking mentorship to enhance your knowledge and resilience.

3. Celebrate Small Wins:

Acknowledge and celebrate your achievements, no matter how small. Celebrating milestones can motivate you to keep pushing forward, reinforcing your persistence.

Conclusion

Persistence is a powerful ally on the journey to financial success. By embracing challenges, maintaining focus, and learning from mistakes, you can overcome obstacles and achieve your financial ambitions. In the next chapter, we will explore lifestyle changes that can accelerate your wealth-building process while enhancing your overall quality of life.

Chapter 14: Lifestyle Changes for Fast Wealth: What to Do Differently

Building wealth often requires adopting specific lifestyle changes that align with your financial goals. By making intentional adjustments to your habits and mindset, you can accelerate your path to financial independence. This chapter will explore lifestyle changes that can enhance your wealth-building journey.

Understanding the Impact of Lifestyle Choices

1. How Lifestyle Choices Influence Financial Success:
Your daily habits and choices directly affect your financial situation. Small adjustments can lead to significant savings and improved financial health.

2. Benefits of Intentional Living:

- **Increased Control over Finances:** By being deliberate in your choices, you

can manage your resources more effectively.
- **Enhanced Focus on Goals:** Mindful living fosters a clear understanding of your financial objectives and promotes actions aligned with them.

Key Lifestyle Changes for Wealth Building

1. Practice Living Below Your Means:
Adopt a frugal mindset by living below your means. Focus on essential expenses and avoid lifestyle inflation as your income grows.

2. Automate Finances:
Set up automated transfers to savings and investment accounts. Automating your finances reduces the temptation to spend and allows for consistent wealth accumulation.

3. Prioritize Health and Well-Being:
Investing in your physical and mental health can lead to better long-term financial outcomes. Healthy individuals often have lower medical expenses and can work more efficiently.

4. Cultivate a Growth Mindset:
Adopt a growth mindset that embraces learning and personal development. Emphasizing continuous improvement can help you develop skills and pursue opportunities for advancement.

Building a Supportive Environment

1. Surround Yourself with Positive Influences:
Connect with individuals who align with your financial goals. Engaging with a supportive community can inspire motivation and accountability.

2. Limit Exposure to Negative Influences:

Minimize interactions with people or environments that encourage unhealthy spending or limit your financial aspirations. Instead, seek out those who inspire growth and positive financial habits.

3. Practice Mindful Consumption:

Be conscious of your spending habits, aiming for quality over quantity. Reflect on whether a purchase aligns with your values and goals before making decisions.

Conclusion

Making intentional lifestyle changes can significantly impact your path to wealth. By adopting healthier financial habits and mindsets, you position yourself for success while enhancing your overall quality of life. In the final chapter, we will discuss the importance of setting financial goals and maintaining focus on your journey towards wealth.

Chapter 15: Your Financial Future: Setting Goals and Keeping Focused

Setting financial goals is fundamental to achieving long-term wealth. Clear objectives provide direction and motivation along your financial journey. This chapter emphasizes the importance of goal setting and maintaining focus as you work towards your financial aspirations.

The Importance of Setting Financial Goals

1. Why Set Financial Goals?
Setting specific, measurable, achievable, relevant, and time-bound (SMART) goals clarifies your financial objectives and

creates a roadmap for your wealth-building journey.

2. Benefits of Goal Setting:

- **Increased Motivation:** Having clear goals promotes accountability and motivates you to take actionable steps toward achieving them.
- **Guided Financial Decisions:** Financial goals provide direction in decision-making, helping you prioritize spending, saving, and investment strategies.

Types of Financial Goals

1. Short-Term Goals:
Short-term goals typically span one year or less. They can include building an emergency fund, paying off credit card debt, or saving for a vacation.

2. Medium-Term Goals:
Medium-term financial goals may take one

to five years to achieve. Examples include saving for a home down payment, funding education, or starting a business.

3. Long-Term Goals:
Long-term goals cover a timeline of five years or more. They encompass retirement savings, significant investments, or wealth-building endeavors.

Strategies for Effective Goal Setting

1. Be Specific:
Clearly define your financial goals, including numerical targets and deadlines. Specificity promotes accountability and enhances motivation.

2. Break Down Goals:
Break larger goals into smaller, actionable steps. Create a timeline for each step to track your progress and celebrate achievements along the way.

3. Regularly Review Goals:

Schedule regular check-ins to assess your progress toward your goals. Adjustments may be necessary based on changes in circumstances, spending habits, or new opportunities.

4. Stay Focused:

Maintain focus on your financial goals by visualizing your success and reminding yourself why you are pursuing wealth. Consider creating a vision board or setting reminders that celebrate your objectives.

Conclusion

Setting clear financial goals and maintaining focus are vital components of your wealth-building journey. By defining your objectives and implementing strategies to keep you on track, you can navigate challenges and achieve long-lasting financial success. As you conclude this book, remember that the pursuit of wealth requires dedication, resilience, and a commitment to continuous learning and growth.

Thank you for embarking on this journey with *Quick Bucks: Your Fast-Track Guide to Getting Rich!* With determination and the knowledge you've gained, you're equipped to take actionable steps toward achieving your financial dreams. The path to wealth is not just about making money; it's about creating a life filled with purpose, fulfillment, and financial independence. Stay committed, stay focused, and keep pushing forward—your financial future awaits!

www.ingramcontent.com/pod-product-compliance
Lightning Source LLC
Chambersburg PA
CBHW070351230526
45471CB00006B/2521